This book is dedicated to my teacher, Mrs. Johns

MW01260153

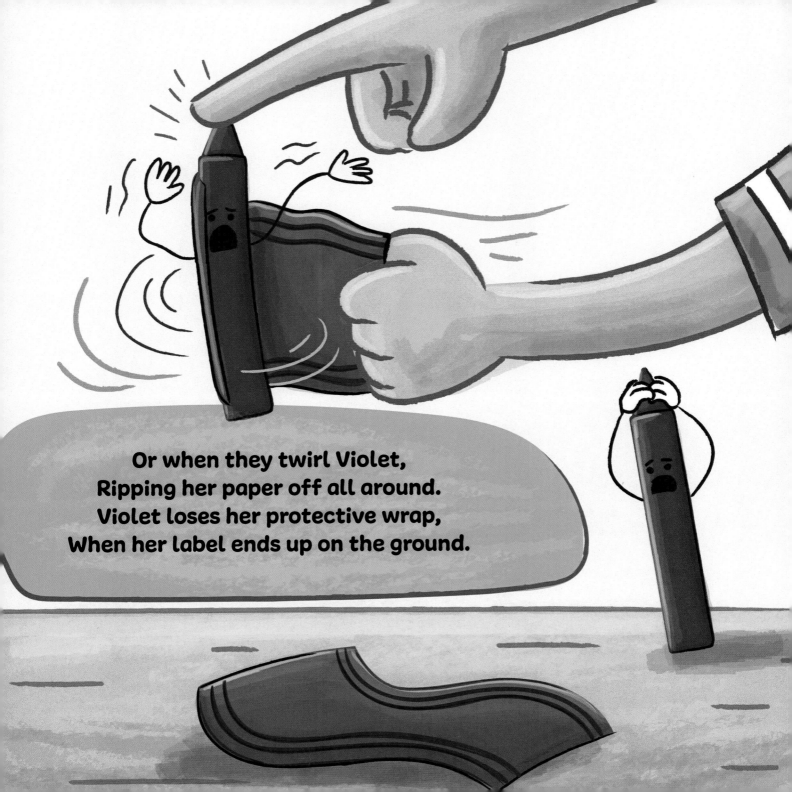

Or when they twirl Violet,
Ripping her paper off all around.
Violet loses her protective wrap,
When her label ends up on the ground.

But Blue may have the worst of it,
Because often he's broken apart into tiny bits.
He's sprinkled across the chair
On which everyone sits.

The worst was when we were left out,
In the windows by the sun.
We were forgotten about in the heat,
Until the day was done.

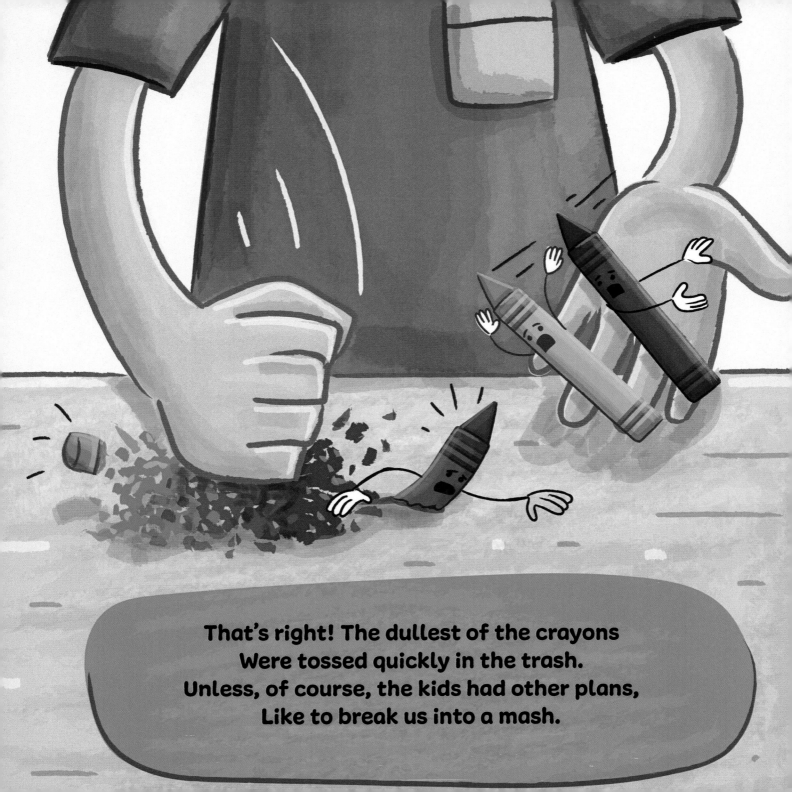

That's right! The dullest of the crayons
Were tossed quickly in the trash.
Unless, of course, the kids had other plans,
Like to break us into a mash.

Well, one day, Yellow had enough and said,
"We won't stand for this anymore!
Come on, crayons! Let's go on strike!
Let's go hide behind the closet door!"

The children were at lunch,
So we had to swiftly act!
They would return from the cafeteria,
And find us missing from the class.

So we headed that way,
Leaving color streaks on the floor.
The children could no longer abuse us.
We would not stand for this anymore!

The kids returned from lunch
And were assigned a coloring task.
"Which colors will you use?"
The teacher asked the class.

The students had to draw their families,
Using as many colors as they could find.
Each was given a blank sheet,
With nothing, not even dots or lines.

Please come back crayons.
Please come back to stay.
We've learned our lesson —
Let's start a new day.

We'll make our classroom
A total "Respectful Zone".
We'll treat our tools with care
So you will feel right at home.

In our supply boxes,
We"ll tuck you neatly away.
So that you will always be there,
And we'll have you each day.

Then we can complete our work,
And it won't be a chore.
We'll respect our tools,
We've learned our lesson and more.

We were so delighted
About the respect and communication.
We were treated from that day on
With much love and affection.

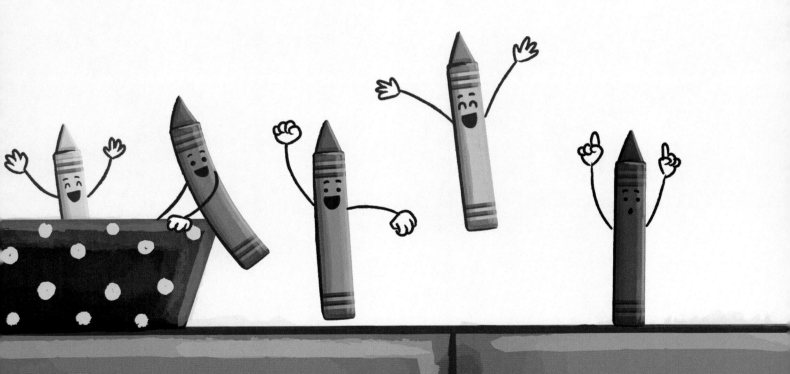

Made in the USA
Las Vegas, NV
10 August 2024

93631531R00021